Protestant Churches

Mandy Ross

Heinemann
LIBRARY

First published in Great Britain by Heinemann Library
Halley Court, Jordan Hill, Oxford OX2 8EJ
a division of Reed Educational and Professional Publishing Ltd.
Heinemann is a registered trademark of Reed Educational & Professional Publishing Limited.

OXFORD MELBOURNE AUCKLAND
BLANTYRE IBADAN JOHANNESBURG
GABORONE PORTSMOUTH (NH) USA CHICAGO

Designed by Tinstar Design
Printed by Wing King Tong in Hong Kong

02 01 00 99
10 9 8 7 6 5 4 3 2

British Library Cataloguing in Publication Data

Ross, Mandy
    Protestant churches. - (Places of Worship)
    1. Protestant churches - Juvenile literature
    I. Title
    280.4

ISBN 0 431 05175 5

Acknowledgements

The Publishers would like to thank the following for permission to reproduce photographs:
Andes Press Agency/Carlos Reyes-Manzo, pp. 12-16, 20; Andrew, Ken. pp. 4, 10; Collections, (Shuel, Brian) p. 19, (Smith, Gary) pp. 6 (inset), 19; Emmett, Phil & Val, p. 8; Format/Roshini Kempadoo, p. 17; Hoffman, David, p. 21; J. Allan Cash, pp. 6, 7, 9, 11, 18; Keith Ellis Arps, p. 5.

Cover photograph reproduced with permission of Robert Harding.

Our thanks to Philip Emmett for his comments in the preparation of this book, and to Louise Spilsbury for all her hard work.

Every effort has been made to contact copyright holders of any material reproduced in this book. Any omissions will be rectified in subsequent printings if notice is given to the Publisher.

Contents

Words printed in **bold letters like these**
are explained in the Glossary.

What is a church?

A church is a building where **Christians** come to **worship** together. Worship means to show respect and love for **God**. Christians believe in God and follow the religion of **Christianity**.

Most Christians in Britain are **Protestant**. There are many different kinds of Protestant **Church**. **Anglican** Christians make up the largest group in Britain. Each kind of Church has a different way of worship, but you can find some things alike in most church buildings.

This church is in Corsack. Many Protestant churches look rather like this.

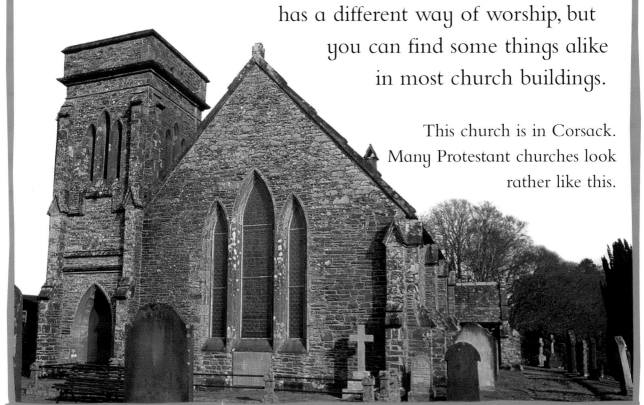

Church and the people

Christians share prayers and all kinds of celebrations in church. The church buildings may also be used for meetings, concerts or youth groups.

This modern church at Milton Keynes was built in 1992.

What do church buildings tell you?

Old or new, grand or simple, in the city or the countryside, no two churches are quite the same.

Looking around a church, you can find out about the people who built and used it in the past, and those who go there today.

Looking outside the church

Churches can be large or small. Some are hundreds of years old, some are new.

Some **Anglican** churches are large and grand. The most important ones are called cathedrals. Most other kinds of **Protestant** church are built more simply.

Some churches have interesting features, like this gargoyle (stone carving).

Lincoln Cathedral in Lincolnshire.

The churchyard

Many churches are set in land called a churchyard. Here there may be graves where **Christian** people are buried after they die. Gravestones tell who is buried there and when they died.

Walk quietly around a churchyard and you may see some birds or animals – quiet, tree-lined churchyards can be a safe place for wildlife.

This simple **chapel** is in Nantmel, Wales. You can see gravestones standing beside it.

What's inside?

Some churches are richly decorated inside. Others are plain and simple.

Most churches have an open area in the centre where people sit in seats, or pews. In **Anglican** churches, this area is called the nave.

The seats are usually in rows, facing the front of the church. The **minister** may stand at the front to lead the **worship**. Some churches face east, pointing towards Jerusalem.

Jerusalem is important to **Christians** because they believe it was where **Jesus**, the son of **God**, died and came to life again two days later.

When people come to church they may sit on long benches called pews, looking towards the front of the church.

Walls and ceilings

Hundreds of years ago, many churches were decorated with brightly coloured wall-paintings. Often they showed stories from the **Bible**, the Christian **holy** book, to teach people who could not read. Now, though, the walls are usually plain.

Churches often have beautiful, high wooden ceilings. In some very grand churches the ceiling may be carved in stone. Lie down on your back for a really good view!

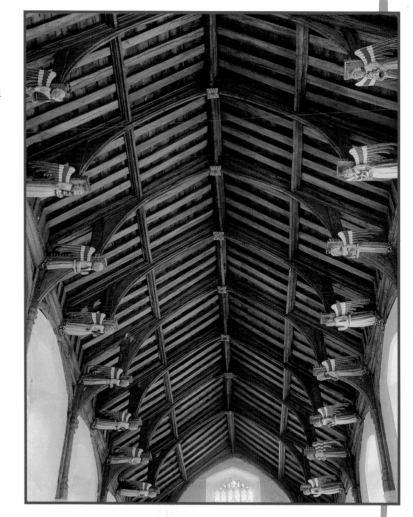

This carved wooden ceiling at South Creake in Norfolk has lots of beautifully painted **angels**.

Things to look for

At the front of most churches you will see a special table called an altar. The altar is used during **worship**.

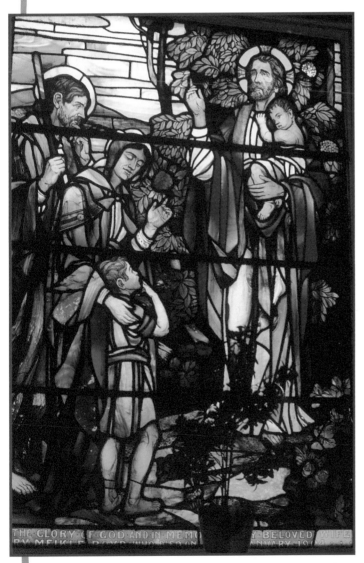

In some churches there may be a raised stand, called the pulpit. The **minister**, or the person who leads the worship, stands in the pulpit so that everyone can see and hear.

You will find a **Bible** on a special desk called a lectern. Near the door, look to see if there is a font. A font is a basin which holds water used for **baptisms**.

Beautiful stained-glass windows brighten the church. Some show stories from the Bible.

Art in church

In every age, **Christians** have made works of art to remember people they loved, or to make their church beautiful. Look for paintings, wall-hangings or carvings. Some may have been made a long time ago.

Many churches are decorated with banners. These are pictures sewn onto large pieces of cloth. They may show the church or the **saint** that the church is named after. They are often carefully embroidered.

This **tomb** inside a church was carved in 1556. It shows two brothers who died, lying side by side.

Who works there?

Most **Protestant** churches, although not all, have a **minister** or leader. He or she leads the **worship**, and works with people who use the church or live nearby. Some ministers work at more than one church.

Other people may work in the church too, for instance helping during worship, or running a youth club.

People who use the church may help to clean and decorate it, and to look after the churchyard. They may also help to raise money to pay to keep the church in good repair.

A minister working with children in a church in Coventry.

Music makers

Making music is an important part of worship. There may be a **choir** made up of children or adults. Choirs often lead the singing. Many churches have an organ, which can make music with lots of different sounds. Someone may play the piano or . guitar and some churches even have a band.

These musicians are leading the singing in church.

Bellringers

If the church has a tower with bells, then bellringers may ring them to celebrate special events such as weddings, or on Sundays to call people to church.

Worship in the church

Christians meet to **worship** together in church on Sundays, and sometimes on other days too. A meeting for worship is often called a **service**.

There are many different kinds of **Protestant** worship. In most church services, Christians say prayers to **God** and to **Jesus**. They also read from the **Bible** and sing special songs called hymns.

In some services, Christians pray silently together. In others, like this one, they sing and may even dance as part of their worship.

Sermons

A sermon is a special talk. It is usually given by the **minister** or another leader in the church. Sermons are usually about Christian teachings, to help Christians lead good lives.

Celebrating Communion

Celebrating **Communion** is an important part of worship. Protestant Christians say special prayers and share bread and wine to remember the last meal Jesus ate with his friends before his death.

It is an important step when a Christian starts taking Communion.

Special days

The important stages of **Christians'** lives are marked at church.

In most **Protestant** churches, a new baby is welcomed into the church by being **baptized**. Some churches baptize adults as well.

When people are old enough to understand what it means to be a Christian, they may take part in a special **service** in which they promise, or confirm, that they will live as Christians. This service is called **confirmation**.

A **minister** baptizing a child using water from the font.

Weddings

Weddings are happy celebrations of love between a man and a woman. Many Christians choose to get married in church. Family and friends come to a special service in which the couple promise to love and care for each other in their life together.

Funerals

Funeral services are held at church when a Christian dies. People meet to pray for the person who has died, and to remember his or her life.

A wedding party poses for photographs outside a church.

Festival celebrations

Throughout the year, **Christians** celebrate many festivals at church. Easter and Christmas are two important festivals.

Easter

Easter is in the spring. On Good Friday, Christians remember how **Jesus** died. Then on Easter Sunday, they celebrate how Jesus rose from the dead to a new life with **God**. Jesus died on a cross. That is why Christians use the sign of a cross.

People give chocolate Easter eggs as a gift at Easter.

Long before Jesus's time, eggs were thought to be special, because they hold life inside them. Eggs became a part of Easter celebrations, as a sign of Jesus's new life.

Advent and Christmas

Advent means 'coming'. It is the name for the four weeks before Christmas when Christians think about the coming of Jesus. Children open advent calendars to remind them that Christmas is coming closer.

At Christmas Christians celebrate Jesus's birth. The church is decked with candles, holly and decorations for this happy festival.

At Christmas, children often act in a play telling the story of Jesus's birth. This is called a nativity play.

Churches are busy places

Churches are often busy places. You can find out about what is going on by looking at the noticeboard in the church or the porch.

Many churches run playgroups for babies and toddlers, or youth clubs where young people can enjoy games or discos. Children may go to Sunday School in the church to learn about **Jesus** and stories from the **Bible**. Some churches run clubs for old people too.

Busy children working on a project at Sunday School.

A fairer world

Jesus taught that it is important to care about other people. So many **Christians** work hard to make the world a better place.

Some offer food or help to homeless people. Others raise money for people in need by holding a jumble sale or a summer fair at church.

Many churches work with people in poorer countries too. For instance, they might buy tea from a fair-trade project, which pays the tea-growers a fair price.

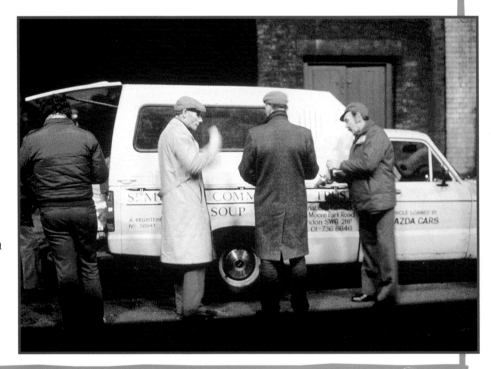

Christians from Saint Mungo's church in London use this van to take food to homeless people.

Glossary

The letters in brackets help you to say each word.

angel Christians believe that an angel is a spirit or being that works for God

Anglican member of the largest Protestant Church in Britain. The Queen is the head of the Anglican Church.

baptism (BAP-tiz-um) special service when someone joins the Church. This may also be called a christening service.

Bible (BY-bull) Christian holy book. The part called the New Testament tells about Jesus's life.

chapel place of Christian worship, often a simple building or a side room in a church

choir (KWIRE) group of singers

Christian (KRIS-tee-AN) someone who follows the religion of Christianity

Christianity (KRIS-tee-AN-i-tee) the religion followed by Christians. Christians believe in God, and they believe that Jesus was God's son.

Church when Church is spelt with a capital C like this, it usually means a group of Christians who share the same beliefs, not a building. (The box at the end of page 23 tells you about some of the main Protestant Churches in Britain.)

Communion (kom-YOO-nee-un) when Christians eat bread and drink wine to remember Jesus and his teachings

confirmation service held in some churches. This is when people make for themselves the promises that were made for them when they were baptized as babies.

God Christians believe that God is a spirit who made, sees and knows everything

holy means respected because it is to do with God

Jesus Christians believe that Jesus was the son of God

minister someone who leads worship and works with people who go to church or live nearby. The minister may also be called a vicar or priest.

Protestant (PROT-ess-tunt) the kind of Christianity which broke away from the Roman Catholic Church over 400 years ago. Roman Catholics follow the Pope as their Christian leader, but Protestants do not.

saint Christians who lived an especially good life. Saints were very close to God when they were alive.

service meeting in church to worship God

spirit Christians believe a spirit is a being who is alive but who does not have a body

tomb (TOOM) stone box for the dead to be buried in

worship (WUR-ship) show respect and love for God

Some Protestant Churches

The **Anglican Church** is the largest **Protestant** Church in Britain. The Church of England, the Episcopal Church in Scotland, the Church in Wales, and the Church of Ireland all belong to the Anglican Church.

There are many other Protestant Churches, which do not belong to the Anglican Church. Some of the larger ones are the Methodist, Baptist, Pentecostal and United Reformed Churches, and the Church of Scotland.

Index